Heads *or* Tails

CARLOS HARLEAUX

peauxeticexpressions.com

Book Cover Design by Matt Davies
Photography by Chris Booth
Typesetting by Stewart A. Williams

ISBN – 13: 979-8-218-13185-2

Printed in the United States

Harleaux, Carlos
Heads or Tails

Published by 7th Sign Publishing

INTRODUCTION

Life is about choices. As I approach nearly four decades of life at the time of this publication, those choices don't get any easier. The consequences are more severe. The victories are sweeter. Our greatest decisions usually boil down to two choices: yes or no, give or receive, love or hate, fight or flight.

Most decisions have two sides of the coin. Some decisions cannot be redone and we must sit in the consequences. Don't mistake that there are some consequences that leave us feeling like we're sitting on cloud nine. There's a surreal element of fear and favor that hovers over many decisions we make.

As with many of my books, *Heads or Tails* inspired itself. I didn't choose to write this book. I had to. This book was necessary to purge, celebrate, grieve and illuminate specific experiences that have happened in my life. My hope is that you see yourself within some of these poems. My prayer is that these poems encourage you to heal, release, go after your dreams and step out on faith to make the difficult decisions.

Heads or tails? Which one would you choose? Walk through the journey with me and see yourself in the choices given. Each poem's "Heads" or "Tails" version is listed side by side for easier judgment, comprehension and pure enjoyment.

BLEACH

Look at us
Covered in the dye, geometrical shapes
That look like pleasing enigmas
To the naked eye
But we know the stories behind their placement
We splashed a little here and there
Not knowing the effect
They would have on the sleeves of our hearts
And the cloaks that clothed our
Calamity that lies beneath
We slipped and slid on the liquid
That doused the floor
Until we fell to the ground
Against our will
The potent fill of the aroma
Ruins our ability to smell the roses
But they're stained anyway
The toxicity of the splatters
Peel sections of our skin away
Yet, to them, our mayhem has become
Their masterpiece

BLEACH

Two woven fabrics
Initially untouched by
The splatters that now decorate
Their surfaces
With no rhyme or reason
They see a calculated mess
That doesn't quite gel
We even left some of the grit untouched
So they could see the difference
Between our reality and
The fantasies we've strewn across the surface
They are involuntarily intoxicated by
The pungent fragrance that reveals our
Fight to fall again
To us it's a sweet, invigorating aroma that
Now feels like home
Despite the fumes
We soon resumed to end in gloom
Yet we love it
No matter how much they question our judgment

FULL MOON

Searching for a sign or
Semblance of sanity
Clarity seems many galaxies away
I try not to let my thoughts lead me astray
Yet here I am smoking ashes to a
Fire that has long since been smoldered
Somebody pass me an ashtray
Is it a penny heads up?
Not splitting a pole to keep our heads up?
I'm usually not this superstitious
My intentions were never fictitious and
That's all that I can say
We've reached a wall of all we can convey
There's a full moon lighting up the sky tonight
Maybe it's a sign that we've lost the love
We once so passionately craved

FULL MOON

The gravitational pull is irresistible
So unpredictable to imagine such
An electric connection
You know my next move before I make it
As I do yours
Let me pour into you and
Chase everything that overflows with
These two lips
Don't loosen your grip
The night sky seems to drip
Its mystery all over us
I don't mind unless you do
There's got to be a logical explanation for
This unrestricted inclination
Look up
It's a full moon
Pulsating as we do

STICKY

You're stuck with me now
That's a frighteningly beautiful notion
What kind of potion
Did you put in my cup?
I'd had enough of love
Yet here I am licking my fingers
Yearning for the next taste
To-go box please
I want to take you home with me and
Greedily devour you from the passenger seat
Is that too much to be or
Do you find yourself
All messy and sticky like me?

STICKY

Just when I say I'm done
My feet get stuck to the
Same pavement I briskly
Glided across
It's plain to see I'm accosted by
Your love or infatuation of the sort
Logic fades where
Head vs heart battles remain
Who will win?
Where do I begin.....again?
I hear the wet resistance crunching
Underneath my sole
Ingrained in my soul
It seems I can't unbind
Let me press rewind and see
How I became so sticky to you

PUDDLE

Where did we go wrong?
We once seemed to walk on water and
Bankhead bounce to a slinky groove
Like TLC did back in '95
Now our eyes are lifted high to the heavens
Hoping for reprieve
Standing in puddles of our own tears
What started as a few drops and then a splash
Has become more than an ocean to endure
We were once so pure before we
Let love's bumps and bruises
Tarnish our hearts
The love is still there and will never die
But these puddles have risen way too high
Aren't you tired of flipping your pillow
To the dry side?
Aren't you tired of hiding red eyes?
I know I am exhausted from the water works of it all

PUDDLE

I come in peace and
Only to leave you leaking
Melt you down and
Sop you up
Like a biscuit
Don't need no jelly
Just need your arms around me
Squeeze me
Love me
You've got me
Truly
I come in peace and
With the intent to surround you
With deep puddles of love
That move between your toes and
Wash against your ankles
Cooling to the touch
It's more than a hunch
That you've got my heart
Drenched with your love

CLENCHED

I sleep with my teeth gritted
Awaken with my hands balled in fists
My ego throws fits since
I'm out of control of how you make me feel
Release the tension, they say
Head up and relax your shoulders, they say
It all seems like empty routines with
Broken promises that start from within
Can't massage it away
Can't meditate it away
I pray it has a short-lived stay
My heart is clenched
Drenched in disappointment
These restraints need to be loosened
One knot at a time

CLENCHED

Thank you for helping me loosen
The grip that once made me slip
Into an abyss and miss the
The chance to live freely
Restraints that you bind yourself to
Are the hardest ones to break
We make the mistake of thinking we can
Undo the damage on our own
I look above and know
You knew better than I
Thank you for your wisdom to
See around the corner
Down the street and
Across the highway to
A road less traveled
A destination where I can
Find pardon
Relieved
I owe it all to you

YELL

I wanna scream it across the ocean and
Cause a ripple effect across the water
Make the earth quake a little
To let everyone know
This beautiful burning inside
You sparked this flame
Pray you don't smother it
This volume is usually reserved for
Frustration and heartache
Not today
My vocal cords resonate
Through the halls that once
Left a flickering light for a sign
That someone was home

YELL

I wanna turn up the tweeter
Push past the meter from my
Diaphragm and post it on Instagram
Letting everyone know how much
I hate you......today
I said I'd never be here
Yet here I stand
Screaming inside while my expression
Holds more grace than Lady Gaga's poker face
I won't give you the satisfaction of knowing
How you've got my insides boiling
I'll yell it in silence instead

LOVE YOURSELF MORE

I changed your name to Ain't Shit
So when you call, it will remind me to
Love yourself more
He is I and I am him
These emotions are filled to the brim and
Overflown is an understatement
Feet to the pavement
Moving forward chanting
Love Yourself More
I repeat the words so much until
My mouth becomes sore
How could it have been a chore to love more?
Don't answer that
I have you blocked anyway
This one hurts to the core

LOVE YOURSELF MORE

Like a kid falling off a bike
Without training wheels for the first time
I'm prime picking
At least that's what I say as I
Remind me to love myself more
That's the very thing
Finding someone with all those
Idiosyncrasies that drove me insane
Someone who absorbs all the pain
You used to tolerate
Love Myself More?
Am I kidding me?
I must stand on this ground
No matter how shaky it trembles beneath
I may never find another better
But at least I loved myself more

HEADLIGHTS

I am enamored when
Your beams dance across my ceiling
Eager with anticipation
Overflowing without trepidation
No hesitation to
Undress you with my eyes
Whether inside these four walls or
Underneath the night sky
They'll all be in awe of
How we thrive
These motions are not contrived
When the headlights turn off and
The quiet hum of the motor stops
My palpitations turn on
My anxiety runs on
Come on in
The door is unlocked

HEADLIGHTS

The beams dance across the ceiling
Awakening the night and
My countless insecurities inside
Simultaneously offering rays down
Memory lane and
A portent to run away
When the quiet hum stops
I still let you in
Despite my hesitation
You can smell my consternation
I let you in despite
The unsavory summation of
Events that have transpired
Turn the headlights off
I don't need them shining light on
My lack of better judgment
The door is already unlocked

LEAVE THAT HERE

Usually I'd say
Pick up your feelings and
Let the door hit you
On your way out
Adios
But this time it's different
Though my grandiose elusiveness
May suggest otherwise
I can't allow you to leave like this
You won't get to ride into the sunset
With my secrets and shit
Of the like
How am I gonna sort through
All these blurry colors and the whites
Without you?
But I don't need you
I'll be just fine
Like I always am
Scram, why don't you?
Just leave the sacred things I shared
At the door
They still belong to me
Now, let yourself be free

LEAVE THAT HERE

I know it hasn't been that long and
You don't usually do this
Neither do I but
I can't contain it
Somehow I'm ok with it
So why don't you lay down
Your cool on the coat hanger
Set those fears on the floor
Let those doubts crawl towards
Every open edifice and find their way out
This positive energy is blinding
Binding even
So let it gel and stick wherever it may
I won't look through your fears and faults
Leave them right where you let them rest
They've been tired of running
All this time
I know you are too

LET'S BUILD

Ain't it funny how the very thing
That took so many stacked bricks to complete
Came crashing down
Like a wrecking ball swinging through
The night life sky
We'll say we didn't see it coming
But the truth is we heard the rumblings
All along
We just thought love was enough
To outrun the inevitable
Here we are, crumbled
Standing face to face
Too exhausted to plead my case
So let's just rebuild, separately

LET'S BUILD

You give me renewed hope
To reconvene
Stacking these bricks from a
Crumbled wall
One by one again
To build something
Fresh and new
Revise the destruction and
Intentions left askew
Don't let this construction be in vain
Don't let me be wrong again
If things fall apart
Can I count on you to get me?

FALL

I tried letting it ride
Coolin on the wave of
Nonchalant situation-ships
Since I had no time for a new relationship
Tell me what's your secret to make me fumble
Stumble and second guess
My best efforts are merely that
Futile attempts to convince myself
You're no different than the rest
Your timing couldn't be worse
But I guess that's the way this thing
Called love goes
Not saying I am
Not saying I'm not
Yet leaning over the fence of
Slipping into you
Is it worth the plunge?
Soaking up your energy like a sponge and
Hoarding it all to myself
Putting it in safe keeping
That must mean you got me
That must me I gotta be
Inexplicably, undoubtedly
Fallin for you
So, you gonna catch me or not?

FALL

I can't remember when it all
Came crumbling to the ground
I look around at my feet and
All I see is shambles of we
Do you know where we went wrong?
Did you see it all along?
All the reasons fall on our heads
Like raindrops from the sky
We prayed to the most high
Yet we are still left with unanswered questions
Why?
Our meteoric rise
Never prepared me for
This devastating fall

SPELL

L-O-V-E
A feeling that grows stronger
Than we can contain
We smile through the pain
Through all of the disdain
Who needs broken hearts?
A-P-A-R-T
Getting through the unfamiliar feeling
Breaking through the comfortable familiarity
We intertwined for all this time
Finding a way to break the cycle
With minimal damage
T-O-G-E-T-H-E-R
Whether near or far
The connection still remains
This spell seems everlasting
What did you cast on me?

SPELL

You give me cause to pause for peace
With a smile that
Makes the chaos
In my head cease
Please sprinkle me with
Your summer rain
I'll do my best
Not to bring you pain
Don't refrain from sharing the
Secret you've put on me
But I understand if that's
Too much to ask
Though I tread with caution
My mind races gallantly
With excitement
If I could just get out of my head and
Step into what I feel when
I arise in the morning when
My feet touch the ground
Straight out of bed
If you are worried 'bout where
I been or who I saw....
Well, you know the rest and
Just know that you got me

PRESCRIPTION

Doctor, what you got to
Induce illusions of grandeur?
Something to wake me up once
This nightmare subsides
I'm not in denial
But no matter how I try
The inscription lays emblazoned
All over my mind
Let me come behind the counter
I'll get it myself
I'll medicate myself
Since you won't
Ignoring better judgment
Holding on to grudges that
Only add extra lines to my hands
There's the remedy
Just let go

PRESCRIPTION

I guarantee you'll never find a
High like this
No cap
Euphoria envies us to
Glide so smoothly like this
They wanna bottle it
They wanna capture it
We feel no need to explain it or
Cause to contain it
That prescription can't be filled
This is a blissful
Intangible state of mind
They couldn't catch us
If they tried

DRIP

Let's slow this drip to
Still waters
I still love you but
I'm growing weary of
The flow of us
We go from full blast to
Low pressure
How dare we have
The audacity to rust
Our trust
The nagging drip of revisiting
Our position is making me dizzy
I'm tipsy and begging to be sober
It's time we flip this coin over and
Take our chances with fate
This drip is driving me insane

DRIP

The steady flow is not enough
I want to be flooded by you
The time and space between these
Droplets has me fawning
I can't believe
I'm this comfortable letting you
Drown me
Maybe I shouldn't give you this
Much credit to save me
Drip drop don't stop
Give me more
Drip drop don't stop
Somebody turn this faucet
On full blast
Put my face under it
Let me consume it
This drip ain't enough
I'd rather you drown me instead

RESERVATIONS

You say throw them out the window
Yet I say I need to keep them close
How I wish I could release
These reservations
But our history has given cause to
Hesitation
Questioning every action and
My equal and opposite reaction
These forces repel
Where they once gelled
Lead feet keep me from
Running back to you
A hardened heart
Prevents it from reopening to you
I'm on empty
Stranded in the state of our current truth

RESERVATIONS

Let's dive in
With you I'm unafraid
With you I'm overjoyed
Inhibitions destroyed
Free to feel and
Feeling me again
Spending time with you is
Reminiscent of a love
I never once knew
Is it true?
Time will tell
I have no reservations
Void of hesitation
I hope you don't mind
I made a reservation for you
Party of one
Let me show you to your table

CHECKIN' OUT

I'm not pulling out of us
Though I can't make you see the
Future with my telescope
I see hurt in our future if we keep
Striving for the stars
I wish I had your persistence
How I wish I had your faith
It's not heavy enough to
Pull the both of us
It's not solid enough to
Seal the fluid doubt of mine
That seeps through the cracks
You call it checkin' out
I call it checkin' in with me
Finally
It's not about me preventing you
From taming me
No blame gaming
Intention shaming
Only healing

CHECKIN' OUT

I feel your eyes burning the back of my head
Maybe it's because mine are wandering to
Find their way back to you
Could it be true that
This electric connection is more
Than a mere spark?
Time will tell if the brush
Of each stroke we make
Will culminate into a
Breathtaking piece of art
Beyond simple hellos and
How are you's
Watching you
Watching me
So are we just gonna
Keep checkin' out or what?

NOSTALGIA

I've seen you before
In another dimension
Not to mention
I know your next phrase
Before the sweet melody plays
In my ear
Your presence feels so familial
Like that corner of the couch
That fits me just right
How have you already infiltrated
The walls I have yet to present to you?
Maybe it's deja vu
Maybe worth making a move
One step closer into your
Nostalgic abyss

NOSTALGIA

The scent of your favorite meal
Sends me down a tailspin
The color matches my bleeding heart
Each time a new memory pricks it
Like that comfortable rocking chair
Imprint nestled into the cushion
No matter how I coach myself
To keep on pushing
You creep into my dreams
Your favorite song plays
All these memories splayed
Across my comforter
Ironically they bring me no comfort
Only a bitter nostalgia

BUTTONS

I was covered to the neck
Until you made me undone
Took your time and loosened
Each insecurity one by one
Tell me your secret please
How did you crack the code to
What others couldn't unlock
With such gentle ease?
Let me help you unfasten them
Now that you've made me comfortable
Now that you've proven yourself
I'll let you take the last one
Now I stand
Naked
I hope it was worth the reveal

BUTTONS

I tell you not to push them
Yet you make no haste to press
May I suggest you don't say things that way?
If and when you do
My words and actions become foul play
You say I'm no good and
Nothing of the sort can come from me
It's your fault for igniting the fire
It's my fault for not extinguishing it
I guess it's true when they say
The ones you love most
Have the greatest power to get under your skin
Don't push me

RAIN

I prayed for you
I longed for you
I waited for this day for
You to wash over me
Cleanse me with your
Rhythmic droplets
Hide my tears
Rinse my fears until
They are diluted to the state
Where only my purpose surfaces
I yearned to dance in your presence
Even as the wind gusts swiftly
Even as the lightning strikes brightly
Even when the thunder claps loudly
What took you so long to
Divert my attention?

RAIN

I thought you'd come to save me
Dilute my pain
Erase the stain of hurt
From yesteryear but no
You're here to bring the wrath
The full typhoon
There is no room to
Break through this cocoon
Engulfed by the rising waters
You said you wouldn't pour down
Like this
You promised you wouldn't
Drown my love but
Let it breathe freely
I thought you'd come to
Ride the wave

THE NEEDLE

The anxious silence fills the room
Before the needle lowers on
The intricate wax
I've let this record spin
Countless times and yet
I still play it back
Everyone else is sick of the tune
But I explore new possibilities
With every listen
I endure the painful moments
Although I shouldn't
I curate the bliss
That fails to exist
Although you seep through the speakers
To speak to me and say
It's not that simple
It is
That simple
In this moment
In this song
Let me live in my
Beautifully twisted fantasy

THE NEEDLE

Don't you let that point
Touch the wax without me
Don't start this groove unless
You really know how to move me
Euphoria under orange lights
A celebratory state of
Future reminiscent to
A time when all we cared about
Was the cool breeze dancing
On our skin
Some memories black as the night
While others glow with a
Blinding fluorescence
Little did we know
We were living in the times
We'd love to embrace again
With open arms

NOPE

How could you tell me no?
Push me to the side to be
Disregarded like a bowl
Full of slimy okra
Can’t you see it’s me?
Don’t you remember me?
I never thought we’d arrive
At this destination
You never used to kiss me
With hesitation
I’m going to make you reconsider
The steam on the windows will fade and
Things will become much clearer
You watch and see

NOPE

My no is not meant to be disregarded
It is not meant to be dissected for
It's possible double negatives
It is not a no that means maybe that
Can be persuaded to a yes
Please understand
My restraint is not easy
When the battle of the
Heart and mind collide
I tried to bend it
Twist it, flip it and deconstruct it
I even threw it up to my ceiling to
See what would stick
But to no avail
Even if I'm wrong
Even if it means I fail
My no is simply that
Nope

BUSY

Leave a message at the beep
I'm unavailable to speak
I need you to let me breathe
You were once my
Sugar honey iced tea
But we've slurped the last sip
Of what we could be
So I can't come to the phone
Don't mean any harm
When I say I want to be alone
If it's anything related to me, you and we
I don't have the heart or the time
I'm just too busy

BUSY

I'm not asking for a complete halt
Just a yellow light to slow down and
Breathe with me
Be with me mentally
Not just physically
You're right next to me but
At times you feel miles within reach
I know you've got things to do
But we're also overdue
Is it that you're too busy
Or has your heart found a new home?
I can handle that
More than the excuses that
No longer hold their weight
Let's make the time for love
Before it's too late

GLASS

It's unfortunate I have to
Cross this threshold
To free myself of your chokehold
The shards jab my sole
Isn't it ironic that each step
Inflicts the pain that
Frees my soul?
The sound of conquered fears
Crush beneath me
Crimson banners blanket my path
Where others have walked before me
If you can catch me before
I reach the other side
You deserve to have me

GLASS

You propelled me right through it
You didn't rest until you saw to it
I thought I'd break it
During my ascension
But you effortlessly lifted the ceiling
I've never tasted air like this
The rise of freedom
Levitation to pure bliss
Kiss the sky
With you by my side
Breaking through the glass
With no scars in sight

DAGGERS

We pull them
Where they pricked us
In our side
Here comes another one
No sooner than the agony
From the last one subsides
Whether intentional or subliminal
Their affect shows no mercy
Blood trickles out of us
As we try to plead our case
Gently at first
Then violently
The toxicity of it all
Makes me want to crawl
In a corner and hideout
Until this storm is over
We aimed them at each other
So carelessly
Now we're reaping
All the benefits and war wounds
Of what we've thrown

DAGGERS

I'll be gentle and remove them
One by one
At the point of insertion
Careful inspection
No matter how painful
The introspection
I'll be there to feed you
Positive affirmations
You are beautiful
You are healed
You deserve to be loved
To be honest
The scars from the daggers
Only enhance your beauty
Truly, nothing can keep you down

BOOMERANG

I wondered if you'd come back
If you'd remember that sweet
Sticky feeling we shared yet
Neither one of us could claim
I wondered if you ever knew
You really held the key for a time
But you never used it
Maybe it was fear
Maybe I never did it for you
That way
I wondered if you played
That game purposely or
If you were aloof to
Stringing me along
Deep down I think you knew
That's just fine because
While it lasted
Whatever "it" was
I certainly enjoyed the ride
It's you again
But it can't be me
Playing the fool again

BOOMERANG

I'd love to bring it back again
Give it another spin
Ride on the waves of chance and
Watch us ride into the sunset
Yet, my caution keeps me bound
I've tried to psyche myself out and
Say it's just a phase I'll fly through
Yet, I'm still filled with that
Hollow feeling
It really sends me reeling
Though you can't see it
I want it so bad I can taste it
You are holding on to me now
Yet, I know your grip will one day
Loosen and let go in the worst way
Just as you believe I've done to you
In that moment, the climax of suspense
Will crescendo until emotions flow like an
Erupting volcano
Flowing over the rocks and mountains
Melting the harsh words I spewed
I just pray I don't want you back by then

HIDE N SEEK

If I secured it in bubble wrap
With countless rubber bands
Could you find your way through?
Would you have the patience to
Pop all the obstacles along the way and
Peel back the layers to uncover me?
If I hid it in a treasure chest
Buried at the bed of the sea
Would you dive in head first
Amidst the wild life and
Dig until you found me?
If I kept it covered in ice
Would you chisel it all away
Or wait in hopes that the
Burning passion would melt it away and
Reveal me to you?
It's true I've hidden my love
In the most compromising spaces and
Cramped places
But you've always been up for the task
To seek no matter how much I hide

HIDE N SEEK

I know you grow weary
Of trying to find me
A complicated lock that
Keeps changing the combination
I don't mean to be such a labyrinth
I don't mean to be such a disaster
But you get me
You understand me
Peeking around the corner
Because I'm afraid of
Revealing all of me
Seems when I do
It makes a fool of me
Thank you for being so strong
Thank you for playing along with
My game of hide n seek

KARMA

What did I do to deserve you?
How many good deeds were racked up
To feel the stacked up intensity
Of your love?
It's so overwhelming and
Sensitive to the touch
Don't you dare pull the plug
Charge me up
Auras of involuntary joy
Wrapped on all sides of me
Like surround sound
No need to keep my ears to the ground
Waiting for the footsteps in the dark
Only the feeling of gliding on air
Sweet melodies in illustrious keys everywhere
What did I do in a past life to get you?
How can I be kind to my future self to keep you?

KARMA

I know what you did last summer
In the back alley
You've got some nerve
Keeping tally
If I exposed all I knew
Their heads would spin
But I stayed true
Unlike you and your
Blasphemous hypocrisy
Disgusting jealousy
You're going to see it
Surely, you're going to reap it
I know what you did and
How it contorts you at night
I'm coming for you
Tell me where you're going to hide
I can't wait to wrap my arms around you and
Squeeze you so tightly

HOT SAUCE

I love the way you dance
On my tongue
Tickling my taste buds
With your special sweet heat
The spicy flavor is one to savor
Don't waste a drop
It's in my favor to find
Such a delectable, peppered flare
I don't need any milk or bread
To cool my senses
I'd rather let you drive me senseless
Shaken for the best effect
What an affect you have on me
I slap their hands when they reach for you
You're mine
They can go get their own

HOT SAUCE

I hate the way you burn my mind
Dousing your fury all over my memories
Until a flame ignites and I can
No longer taste the good ones
What once your secret sauce has
Developed into your potent poison
I do not want a taste
But if I ever make it out of this
I vow to paste reminders everywhere
With color coded coordination and
An official ordination
To never allow myself to
Believe the hype of a flavor
That has since long soured

NMW

No matter what
That's what we said
Like that flimsy wire
Securing the opening of
A loaf of bread
Thick as thieves
Thin as leaves
Promises promises fading
Like New Jack City in the night
We fight for all the ones
We can't keep
I can't sleep and think
I need an Ambien
So I creep
Nah, my conscious would
Make me feel so cheap
Can we afford the cost
Of all the things we said we'd keep?

PEEL

They see an exoskeleton
Too tough to crack
I see a challenge for beauty revealed
If you'll allow me to
Peel your layers back
I understand the need for protection
Seeing you is like looking
At my own reflection
Maybe we can reveal each other
If that's not too indecent
If it's not too much to ask
Exploring all the layers you've
Deemed unpalatable
Incomparable
I love your unique skin
It makes the task that much sweetest
To uncover what's within
It would be a sin to let your
Ripeness go to waste and
Not offer me a taste

PEEL

They all see what I present
No cause to question
What lies deep within
Commence to dig
Beneath the skin
Unravel what few feel
Underneath this peel and
Seek to find
What has settled on
One person's mind
The unpopular opinion
How do they see you?
Would they still care to
Eat the fruit
If they found the contents bruised?
Everyone wants a perfect bite
That doesn't exist
Work on you from the inside out
Inject your purpose
Peel back the doubt

HEADS OR TAILS

My fate lies betwixt
My thumb and pointer finger
No need for pointing fingers
This one's all on me
I'm giving it an honest flip
Wherever it lands is where
The miracle will be
Toss it up
Spin it
Twirl it around
No matter the trick or treat
It's victory or defeat
When it lands face down
Smile or frown
It's mine to own
I might need a shot of Patron
To ease the edge
Get me off the ledge
I'm not ready yet
I'm more prepared than
I ever imagined
Heads or Tails?

ABOUT THE AUTHOR

Carlos Harleaux is an author, poet, blogger, publishing consultant and podcaster (tune into The Water Bearer Podcast on YouTube, Anchor, Spotify, Google Podcasts and Apple Podcasts). He resides in Dallas, Texas. He enjoys creating through writing, live music, outdoor events, traveling and delicious food.

He is the author of several poetry books, including *Blurred Vision, Hindsight 20/20, Honesty Box, Commissioned to Love, Stingrays, Eleven: Things We Never Said,* and *Cataracts.*

Carlos's novels include *Fortune Cookie, No Cream in the Middle, When the Cookie Crumbles, A Swipe in the Wrong Direction, Only for One Night* and *Trigger Pointe.* Plus, read his informative account of independent publishing, *Can I Pick Your Brain?*

Visit peauxeticexpressions.com to learn more about Carlos, purchase his other books, read his blogs and get updates on upcoming projects.

Printed by Libri Plureos GmbH in Hamburg,
Germany